Inspiring
Women
Every Day

September

WRESTLING WITH WISDOM
....
ALEX BROOKS

October

NATURALLY SUPERNATURAL
....
WENDY MANN

MIX
Paper from
responsible sources
FSC® C021017
www.fsc.org

WAVERLEY ABBEY
RESOURCES

Alex Brooks

Alex Brooks is an aspiring fiction author who even as a little child loved writing short stories. She lives in her adopted home of Guernsey with her husband and three sons and has studied Kingdom Theology with Westminster Theological Centre. She co-founded and co-leads a group that meets for monthly quiet mornings, and helps with a small weekly fresh expression of church that is aimed at ex-offenders. She is passionate about faith, theology, writing, mental health and mindfulness, and especially at the points where these intersect with each other.

Wendy Mann

Wendy is part of the King's Arms church in Bedford and runs her own ministry called Wendy Mann Equip. She loves to encourage and empower others to be all they're called to be in God. Wendy enjoys good coffee and connecting with God in nature. Check out her website for more info: www.wendymannequip.org

Copyright © Waverley Abbey Resources 2022.
Published by Waverley Abbey Resources. Waverley Abbey Resources is an operating name of CWR, Waverley Abbey House, Waverley Lane, Farnham, Surrey GU9 8EP, UK. Tel: 01252 784700 Email: mail@waverleyabbey.org
Registered Charity No. 294387. Registered Limited Company No. 1990308.
Front cover image: Adobe Stock Images
Concept development, editing, design and production by Waverley Abbey Resources. Printed in England by Yeomans. All rights reserved. No part of this publication may be reproduced, stored in a retrieval system, or transmitted, in any form or by any means, mechanical, photocopying, recording or otherwise, without the prior permission in writing of Waverley Abbey Resources.
Unless otherwise indicated, all Scripture references are from the Holy Bible, New International Version® Anglicised, NIV® Copyright © 1979, 1984, 2011 by Biblica, Inc.® Used by permission. All rights reserved worldwide.
Other translations: ESV, The Holy Bible, English Standard Version® (ESV®) Copyright © 2001 by Crossway, a publishing ministry of Good News Publishers. All rights reserved; NLT, New Living Translation, copyright ©1996, 2004, 2015 by Tyndale House Foundation. Used by permission of Tyndale House Publishers, Carol Stream, Illinois 60188. All rights reserved.

WRESTLING WITH WISDOM

ALEX BROOKS

Job 1:1–6

'Job… was blameless and upright; he feared God and shunned evil.' (v1)

This month we will be looking at the book of Job. Considered one of the wisdom books (along with Proverbs and Ecclesiastes), it is the **only** Old Testament book not set in Israelite lands or about the Jews. Uz is believed to have been south-east of the land of Israel. Considering that the Old Testament is very focused on God's chosen land and people, this setting of Uz stands out as different, but nevertheless has much to teach us.

We're told Job is upright and blameless. This will be important as we go on further. He was an upstanding citizen by all accounts, and his assets reflected that. Everything has gone right for him, and why shouldn't it? A good family, many herds of cattle, camels, sheep, and a good reputation – he was the 'greatest man among all the people of the East' (v3). If anyone deserved good things happening to them, it was Job. Or – so we think by our human understanding and standards. Our views might well be challenged this month as we go through the book of Job.

Today we are a global society, very different to biblical times. Uz was located at a distance from Israel that may have seemed great back then, but today would be negligible. However, the need to belong, inherent in all of us, pushes us to find others who are like us in some ways. As Christians we may think we understand some of what it means to be God's people, but have we unwittingly judged others as being outside that group?

Are we ready to accept that our perceptions might not be the absolute truth? That we are making our choices and judgments based on a small fraction of the truth...

For Prayer and reflection

Lord, help me see that I don't have the full picture, to trust that You see it all. Help me let go of any biases about who does or doesn't belong in Your story. Amen.

Who's to **blame**?

Job 1:6–12

'Then the LORD said to Satan, "Have you considered my servant Job?"' (v8)

W e're given an image of a heavenly council that mirrors what we understand on earth – a King surrounded by his court. Whether it's real, or imagined for the purposes of the book, it gives us a way to relate to God. You can imagine the meetings, the angels bringing reports to God who then gives out instructions, all as we might read of an earthly court. It's quite the image, isn't it?

Then we have mention of the satan. In this case, **the** satan is correct – the Hebrew here is *ha-satan* – the oppressor, or the accuser or adversary. This is a role, not a name. This ha-satan is a little different to the character we know as Satan, or the devil, in the rest of the Bible. Maybe it's a precursor to the Satan we know elsewhere. Job's version is not inherently evil, but is the one who oppresses, who accuses, who stirs things up, who asks the questions. He has no power here, his purpose is to challenge God. And here he decides to stir things up by bringing attention to Job.

God allows the satan to affect Job, but the suffering is not caused by God Himself. Although we're only at the start of our journey through Job, we can already see from this passage that we can't blame God for everything. Christ was the ultimate scapegoat, although sinless he took on the blame by choice. The satan likes scapegoating people, causing confusion and dissention – whereas Christ *chose* to be the scapegoat for our sins. Sometimes we find ourselves angry and needing someone to be the scapegoat, which is unfair to them. Are there any situations where you want to blame someone just to have a focus for your emotion? Take it to God.

For Prayer and reflection

God, what have I unfairly put at Your door or someone else's when the blame should have landed elsewhere? Forgive me please. Amen.

Weekend

Words of lament

....

Psalm 102:1–11

'Hear my prayer, LORD; let my cry for help come to you.' (v1)

Taking a slightly different but related tack for the weekend, we will be looking at lament. Job does a fair amount of lament – that is, expressing his disappointment and sadness to God. We'll look at his lament separately. The Psalms are full of examples of lament, such as the one we are looking at today. The author doesn't hold back his frustration, using poetic phrases such as: 'My heart is blighted', 'I eat ashes as my food and mingle my drink with tears' and 'I wither away like grass'.

Sometimes we get too used to having the British 'stiff upper lip' ingrained as part of our culture. You may find yourself answering 'I'm fine' when asked how you are, when you might be nothing of the sort. Even if the time and place aren't suitable for offloading to other people, God is always available, and He can take anything we can throw at Him. The benefit of knowing we've been heard – and thus can let go of our frustrations – can't be underestimated.

....

For Prayer and reflection

Take time to write your own words of lament to God, as a prayer, a letter, poetry or a psalm. Don't hold back, tell Him all your concerns.

Everything is **lost**

Job 1:13–22

'The LORD gave and the LORD has taken away; may the name of the LORD be praised.' (v20)

Job is observing the traditional grief rituals here, and so far this is nothing out of the ordinary. His words of mourning match his actions so far, and it looks as though he accepts that the cliché of 'these things happen' is all part of the cycle of life. We come to this earth with nothing, and we leave it with nothing. So, whatever we have gained in the meantime cannot be kept, and Job appears to have accepted that.

When things are tough, we often hold on to the truths we know – that God is for us, not against us (Rom. 8:31), that in all things God works for good (Rom. 8:28), that we can do everything through Him who gives us strength (Phil. 4:13). There are plenty more to choose from. Scripture passages help us focus on God when something threatens to derail us from our path with Him.

Writing our truths down and repeating them helps us remember them when we are in need. Like those times tables we learned in school, repetition helps embed things. And writing our alphabet helps reading become second nature. The more often we read it, write it, see it, use it, the more likely it is to be readily available at the point we need it. When I need something, I don't want to spend long looking for it, I need it at my fingertips, or the tip of my tongue. Firmly in my mind. To wake up to a bad day having encouraging Bible verses to hand can make it a bearable day instead – you may well have a favourite verse for these times. If not, it's worth finding one or more that are meaningful to you. Think of it as a sort of spiritual first aid box.

For Prayer and reflection

What Bible verses are the ones you want to hold on to? Select one or more and write it down – put it somewhere you will see it to engrave it on your heart.

The **gift** of pain

"'Shall we accept good from God, and not trouble?" In all this, Job did not sin in what he said.' (v10)

I t's perhaps easier to accept suffering if we know there's an end point. If we know it's only for a day, a week, a month, we can perhaps bear suffering, knowing it will eventually stop. To not have an end date, and to then have a second round of suffering, must be incredibly demoralising for Job.

However, there is one small chink of a blessing here. This did not happen to him all in one go. Although we don't know the time frame, we can see that there was a gap between the first test and the second. It gave Job time to gain a little strength and adjust to the repercussions of the first test before the second one hit. Sometimes a little time and space can help you gain the strength you need for what may come next. The initial 'fight or flight' reaction passes and we adapt to be ready for the next situation.

Strange as it may seem, pain is actually a blessing. It protects us and alerts us when something is wrong. An infection, an injury, overdoing an activity, are all signs to our body to be aware we need to pause and take note of where we're at. It's a notification to take a break and rest, to visit the doctor, or maybe just to do some stretches the next time we exercise. Some people are born without the ability to sense pain – they may stub their toe and feel nothing – but that means there is no alert system in the body. There is no way of knowing there is a problem somewhere in your body, be it infection, bone breakage or organ failure. When seen like this, maybe a little pain isn't so bad. It keeps us safe.

For Prayer and reflection

God, thank You for the gift of pain. Thank You that it keeps us safe. Have mercy on those who do not feel pain and care for them. Amen.

Holding **space** for someone

'No one said a word to him, because they saw how great his suffering was.' (v13)

For Prayer and reflection

Lord, please bring to mind someone who needs space held for them/ someone who can hold space for me. Prepare that space ahead of me and be with us in that space. Amen.

Job's friends start off well here. They are there for him in the immediate aftermath of his suffering – this has parallels with the Jewish custom of sitting (*shiva*), of mourning for relatives by being with them, supporting and comforting them for a period of seven days. The word *shiva* is the Hebrew word for 'seven' – thus the link with the time period. We can safely assume there will have been traditional mourning rituals in Uz in those times, and Job's friends would have been doing what was expected of them in a time of bereavement. Though Job is not an Israelite himself, he may have been aware of and even practised Jewish rituals, given he is aware of who God is.

Holding space for others – being there for them physically, mentally, spiritually and emotionally, without expectation or judgment, is one of the greatest gifts we can give someone else. If you've ever had someone be there for you like that, you'll know how beneficial it is to feel truly heard. Complete non-judgment, space to let the emotions come up as they will, no problem-solving, just listening... we don't have to be a therapist to be there for someone. Whether we want someone to be there for us, or we want to be there for someone, sometimes just making and holding space is enough. Yes, there are times when it's appropriate to give advice. It might even be asked for! But there's a time to refrain from talking and just listen. Ecclesiastes reminds us that there's 'a time to be silent and a time to speak,' (Eccles. 3:7) – we need God's help in discerning when to speak and when to be silent.

A **wonderful** life

'May the day of my birth perish, and the night that said, "A boy is conceived!"' (v3)

You may have seen the old film *It's a Wonderful Life*. The main character, George Bailey, has had a good life – he has a family and a good job – all is going well for him at the start of the film, but then he has a run of bad luck. Does this sound a little familiar after reading today's passage? George finds himself suicidal, believing everyone would be better off without him and wishing he'd never been born. Clarence, the guardian angel who saves him from his jump into the river, shows him what life would be like if he'd never been born. It turns out that his life had meaning and purpose that he hadn't seen.

Of course, we don't have a guardian angel like Clarence showing up at the right time. And neither did Job. I suspect the book of Job would have read a lot differently if that were the case. Job is merely lamenting and vocalising how he feels. He curses his day of birth but does not curse God through all this.

To be at this point of misery is a tough place to be. It's not somewhere we would choose to be. Even if not in despair, it's common to question our purpose. Who am I? What's my purpose? What's my role, my identity? What's the one special thing that *I* am supposed to do – maybe something that *only* I am suited to do? Does God have a plan for my life, a reason for me being here? I ask these questions myself – I'm still waiting for the answer. But I suspect that the answer is hiding in plain sight and is a lot less complicated than I make it. Maybe it's simply to 'act justly and to love mercy and to walk humbly with your God' (Mic. 6:8).

For Prayer and reflection

Lord, thank You that You have a purpose for me, that my life fits in to Your plan for creation. Help me trust You with this even when it feels like I have no place. Amen.

Did you think to **pray**?

Job 5:8–17

'But if I were you, I would appeal to God; I would lay my cause before him.' (v8)

When you're grieving, the last thing you want to hear is, 'Did you pray about it?' or 'Maybe you should have prayed more' or any number of variations on these phrases. Especially when those friends have no intention of praying themselves and are not speaking directly to God. This is Job's scenario. A bit 'do as I say, not as I do', really, and it seems a little judgmental of them.

Yes, prayer is a help in all sorts of circumstances, and it's certainly a good thing to do – God wants to hear all our thoughts and feelings from us. If it's used as a piece of advice from a friend to someone suffering and grieving, however, it's not quite so helpful – even if well-intentioned. In the first stages of grief we may struggle to put many things into words – words that express clearly our sentiments at that time. Thankfully we have a Holy Spirit who 'intercedes for us through wordless groans' (Rom. 8:26). When we don't have the words ourselves, this is an invaluable aid in prayer – we only need to ask for the Spirit's help.

It's a difficult balance to achieve. When we see a friend suffering, often the first thing we want to do is fix the problem for them. Maybe prayer would help – but it's not necessarily our place to say this. It's so hard to know how to discern what we should and shouldn't say. If one is advising from a place of experience and can discern carefully what to say and when to say it, then with care the right thing may be said, but there is still a chance of getting it wrong. With the help of God's Holy Spirit will we know when to speak, what to say and when to stay quiet.

For Prayer and reflection

Holy Spirit, guide me in discerning when to act or speak, and when to be silent and just listen. Amen.

Weekend

Imaginal cells

....

Romans 8:29–39

'For those God foreknew he also predestined to be conformed to the image of his Son...' (v29)

This weekend we make a slight diversion. Caterpillars and butterflies are rather marvellous beings, aren't they? They come from the same source – each caterpillar has imaginal cells in it, dormant until needed. Not imaginal as in 'imagine', but as in 'image'. Those imaginal cells each contain an image – a blueprint as it were – of what the butterfly will look like.

The butterfly does not present itself without struggles taking place. The caterpillar fights to stay a caterpillar, but the imaginal cells fight to bring the butterfly out. Then the butterfly's struggle out of the chrysalis is what gives it the strength in its wings. We have our own spiritual imaginal cells, containing the image of God.

Just like that caterpillar we change through struggles. We will see those struggles eventually make us who we really are, and who we are meant to be. By struggling through our troubles, we have the chance to see those beautiful butterfly wings for ourselves. Those troubles shape us and make those wings extra beautiful.

....

Optional reading

Margaret Silf, *Hidden Wings* (Darton, Longman & Todd Ltd, 2017).

Risking **friendship**

'How painful are honest words!' (v25)

Job recognises the honesty of the words he has just heard, though Eliphaz has been rather brutal with them. Yet some of what he says may be true. Are there times when we avoid honesty because of fears of how it might affect a relationship? Are we scared to tell the truth for fear of what others might say? To risk that someone will take what we have said and turn it against us or reject us can prevent us from being totally honest. We might end up hedging our words to err on the safe side of not causing insult. It can be a thin line to tread. What friendships do we have that we don't want to risk losing? If we have to lie to keep them, are they really relationships that should be kept?

In the past, I've taken a couple of friends to A&E when they were at crisis point. I told them it was more important to me to have them safe and well and possibly hating me, than to keep the friendship and risk something bad happening. I loved them too much for that to happen, and I was willing to risk ending the friendship over this. Thankfully we are still friends, but I'd do the same again even if the result were different. It was a tough decision, but the honesty paid off.

There are times to speak honestly even if it hurts, though careful discernment is needed. Ephesians tells us we must 'speak truthfully to [our] neighbour, for we are all members of one body' (Eph. 4:25). When the right thing is to speak up instead of remaining silent, we need the courage to act – with the Holy Spirit's guidance. God's Spirit can give us the direction we need to navigate these situations.

For Prayer and reflection

Holy Spirit, put the right words in my mouth and give me the courage to speak up when it's needed. Amen.

Where are you **planted**?

Job 8:11-15

Bildad is the second of Job's friends to speak. He suggests to Job that he turn to God - believing that Job has done something wrong and needs to repent. His words, though wrong in this case, give us pause to consider where we get our spiritual strength from. What soil are we planted in? What everyday things feed our souls, and what drains them?

Can we thrive without the right soil, without water, or will we merely survive? Survival is all very good for certain times, but it does not sustain us. The better our soil, the more frequent the watering, the more resilience we have when trouble hits. The Psalmist describes himself as 'like an olive tree flourishing in the house of God; I trust in God's unfailing love for ever and ever' (Psa. 52:8). This image of an olive tree planted in the temple shows us where we will benefit from being planted – in God's ground, in proximity to His presence. In practical terms, this is somewhere where we will feel spiritually fed. We want to thrive, not just survive.

So, what does our soil look like? In what shape or form does God's presence feed you? It can be prayer, scriptures, meeting together, and much, much more. We each need soil specific to us. My own soil is fed and watered in several different ways; being creative is part of it, as are quiet mornings, and recently, cold water swimming – and much more besides. They all remind me in different ways of God's presence, His creation, His love, and they help me feel alive. What does your own soil look like? Take some time to consider what you're planted in, and what watering you need.

'Can papyrus grow tall where there is no marsh? Can reeds thrive without water?' (v11)

For Prayer and reflection

Father, find me the soil and the water I need to thrive with You. Let me be planted first and foremost in You and watered with Your Spirit. Amen.

Why study with us?

Integrating your faith and your studies: Your faith isn't reserved for Sundays and church. It's part of who you are, and how you live out your profession. All of our courses are underpinned by a Christian ethos and understanding. Be encouraged to integrate your faith into your course, and your professional life beyond.

Flexibility to suit your circumstances: Squeezing in study around your job, your family, and your 101 other responsibilities? We'll make it as easy as possible for you. You can enroll on a course that's taught part-time or online via distance education. We have campuses in Farnham and in Bradford to serve the south and the north of England.

Choose your level: Whether you're studying for the first time, or you're a seasoned academic, you'll find a course at the level that suits you. You can try an introductory course, study a Waverley Award, or delve into a Masters, and anything in between.

Tutors you can trust: Our tutors have years of experience in their fields and many have completed doctoral level studies. You'll hear our tutors on podcasts, or see them contributing to journals and academic discussion. You're learning from the highly-learned.

Learning in community: Join a cohort of like-minded people and be part of the community of learners. Whether you're learning online or in-person, you'll be in touch regularly with your fellow students.

Where you can study

Our vision is to equip people, wherever they're based geographically. That's why we offer courses delivered in the Farnham Campus, Bradford Campus and via distance education.

Farnham Campus

Waverley Abbey House, Farnham, Surrey

Come on site to study any of the courses in the Counselling and Spiritual Formation Faculties.

Bradford Campus

Church on the Way, Bradford

You can study these counselling courses on site in Bradford:

- Introduction to Christian Care and Counselling

- Waverley Certificate in Christian Counselling

- Diploma of Higher Education in Counselling

Distance Education

Study from anywhere in the world with our courses delivered via distance education:

- Contemporary Chaplaincy

New for 2022

- Contemporary Discipleship
- Contemporary Church Ministry

For more info on courses you can study, visit **waverleyabbeycollege.ac.uk**

Job 9:1–19

'He is the Maker of the Bear and Orion, the Pleiades and the constellations of the south.' (v9)

Approachable or unapproachable

We have a description here that gives us a glimpse of wondrous creation and awesome power. You cannot resist God and 'come out unscathed' (v4). He 'performs wonders that cannot be fathomed, miracles that cannot be counted' (v10). You only have to search briefly online for images of deep space and celestial objects to know how vast and varied the universe is – galaxies, stars, nebulae, planets, moons, comets and much more. Even accounting for the poetry of the passage, this paints a big picture of God's creative power.

And yet God appears to be unapproachable. Job can't find a way of making himself heard by God. Sometimes we too find that God seems unapproachable. We find times where it seems we have a wall between ourselves and God. Even Mother Teresa, with all the selfless work she did, had only silence from God for much of her life. Despite all the work she was doing in God's name, she did not feel His presence and felt only an emptiness. Still, like Job, that did not dissuade her from following God for the rest of her days.

When we feel God's absence, it helps to know that we are not alone and that others have also felt that absence. We may not be able to reason why this is. Yet the maker of the constellations, the very ones that we see in the night sky, is still there with us. Just the same way as the sun still shines even when the clouds block it, our Lord is still present even when we cannot feel it. We can have confidence that He is there, has heard us, and is near to us, even when we have no sense of His nearness.

For Prayer and reflection

Thank You, Lord, that even when we find only silence, You are still there, You still hear us. Amen.

Daughter of the King

'Can you fathom the mysteries of God? Can you probe the limits of the Almighty? (v7)

Zophar hears nothing from Job but meaningless words. He doesn't hear anything that makes sense to him, so when it's his turn he speaks up and suggests it's because Job feels guilty. He thinks that he has insight that Job is missing! This is becoming a theme with the three friends. Theology can be useful at times of course, but in these situations, theology is only useful when applied with compassion. Theology without compassion is a fraction of the whole picture. Zophar here gives the perfect example of how NOT to use theology.

As we saw yesterday, sometimes God feels unapproachable to us. Maybe you've grown up with an idea of God as a disciplinarian who sits on a throne far, far away and doesn't have much to do with our everyday life. Maybe you've grown up with a different but equally unapproachable image of God. That makes it harder to approach God but not impossible. This is when scriptures help remind us. Hebrews 4:15 reminds us that 'we do not have a high priest who is unable to feel sympathy for our weakness' – He is with us exactly where we are! Verse 16 goes a step further and tells us we can 'approach God's throne of grace with confidence' – we can step up and approach God knowing that He gives us grace, He always has time for us, and always has space for us.

Although God is majesty incarnate, and sovereign of all, we can approach His throne with the right of inheritance as a daughter of the King. We don't have to wait in line, wait to be summoned, or plead our case with His courtiers before we may enter. We have the right to just enter our Abba Father's presence as a child of God.

For Prayer and reflection

How easy do you find it to approach God? How can you make it easier? Try a different form of prayer, such as writing, singing, creativity, different postures, walking.

Am I **guilty**?

Job 13:7–19

'Though he slay me, yet will I hope in him; I will surely defend my ways to his face.' (v15)

Job's reply to Zophar shows an expectation that God will vindicate him – regardless of what is brought before him he will not stop trusting in God. Where else would he go? Losing his faith is not an option. Even if he is brought to the point of death in these sufferings, he will not give up his faith in God. It is possibly the one thing keeping him going. When all around you is collapsing, you hold on to the things that are not doing so. Job's lost everything else; he won't lose his faith.

When things get tough it often feels like you're hanging on by a very thin rope – one which could break at any moment. Sometimes all we can do is just hold on for dear life. With faith in God comes the reassurance that if you let go, 'underneath are the everlasting arms' (Deut. 33:27). It reassures me no end that on the tough days there are some strong arms there to catch me. Any time, day or night, God will catch you when you fall.

Would you defend God to the last? We are blessed in the West to not be persecuted for our faith, to have the freedom of going to church and meeting with others without worrying about the repercussions. Not all are so fortunate, and many have had to decide whether their faith is worth the cost of losing so much. I recall hearing the question posed years ago: 'If you were in court, on trial for being a Christian, would there be enough evidence to convict you?' I haven't thought about that question in years, but now it brings me to a stop, to examine how I live my life. Would I be found guilty? Do people see Jesus in me and, if not, how can I show Him to them?

For Prayer and reflection

Lord, do I show You to others? Is there enough evidence to convict me? Guide me to how I can show You to others. Amen.

Weekend

Sitting with darkness

....

Psalm 121:1–8

'He who watches over Israel will neither slumber nor sleep.' (v4)

We always think light is good and dark is bad. A lot of language in the Bible reinforces that. However, darkness isn't inherently evil. Night-time isn't bad just because it's dark. Shadows aren't bad because they are dark. Yet so often we are afraid during the night-time, afraid of anything that we can't see. We are so quick to put the house lights on the moment the sun begins to set. There are similarities with our thoughts and feelings. We're quick to allow the happy, content, amazed, peaceful, thankful thoughts and feelings. And we press down any signs of anger, sadness, puzzlement, anxiety – any thought or feeling that has a negative connotation. God is still here in the midst of all those feelings. Even in the darkest part of the night, God doesn't sleep. He doesn't stop his watch over us – he NEVER stops.

Yet, what if we sit with that darkness – not making it worse but allowing it to just *be*. Letting the twilight change to darkness without putting the light on – sit outside and let your eyes naturally adjust to the darkness. Somehow this can make things seem less scary.

....

For Prayer and reflection

Optional reading: Barbara Brown Taylor, *Learning to Walk in the Dark* (Norwich: Canterbury Press, 2015)

Testing, **testing**

Job 23:1–12

'But he knows the way that I take; when he has tested me, I shall come forth as gold.' (v10)

This passage reminds me of Malachi 3:3, 'He will sit as a refiner and purifier of silver...' The oldest way of refining and purifying is done by applying heat, usually in the form of a fire. This burns away the impurities in the silver. Without burning away those impurities it will never be good enough quality. It **has** to go through the fire. BUT, too long in the fire will ruin the silver. So, the refiner has to pay close attention to the silver in order to take it out at the perfect point. Job, whilst frustrated at his inability to get a just hearing from God, has realised that this is what is happening to him. He can see that there will be a benefit to all that is happening – that even if he doesn't know the purpose himself, he can accept that he will come out of this refined and purified.

One more vital point on refining gold or silver – the refiner knows the job is done when he sees his face reflected in the metal. God knows when we have been refined and purified enough when He can see His image reflected in us. We are made in His image (Gen. 1:27), so the core is already there, already in place. It's what's around it that needs to be refined. We have the choice, though – God will never force it on us. He will never make us do anything we aren't ready for, and He will be there watching all the way through.

Testing is tough. It's painful. It's deep. It's going to hurt. However, if we want to become what God intends us to be, He has to go deep in us to make a lasting change. And because we know God, we know that a change He makes is a good and worthwhile one.

For Prayer and reflection

Thank You, Lord, that You don't let us be tested more than we need. Thank You that You are there all through the process, watching till You see Your reflection. Amen.

I have **hope**

Job 19:23–27

'And after my skin
has been destroyed,
yet in my flesh I
will see God…'
(v26)

This is starting to go on and on – the same pain, the same grief, the same suffering – but no end is in sight for poor old Job. He's getting to the end of his tether. The pain has likely become chronic, he can't fathom what it would be like without the suffering, and he can't remember what it's like to feel happy. His friends don't understand him, his wife is judging and rejecting him, all his associates and acquaintances have deserted him. He's been left with nothing. What do you do when you have nothing left?

Yet all is not lost. He has hope. He has certainty that one day he will see God. And that keeps him going. In a time where belief in life after death was perhaps not so well-known, Job had that extra step of faith that maybe no one else around him had at that time. We can have that same certainty too – we can always have hope in God. And that can sometimes be the one thing that keeps us going. Faith that we will see God.

We know that 'these three remain: faith, hope and love' (1 Cor. 13:13). After everything is gone, these three are still to be found. No one can take them away from us – the only one that can lose these is us, ourselves. Even then they're easily retrieved. We can choose to hold on to hope, to faith, to love. We *need* to hold on to these. On a bad day, they'll be there. When we lose someone, they'll be there. When our material possessions are gone, they'll be there. When everything is chaotic, they'll be there. They'll *always* be there. And because they will always be there, we know that God will always be there too.

**For Prayer
and reflection**

**Where is your hope
found? If
everything around
you was gone,
what would you
do? Would you
hope in God? Tell
Him your hopes.**

It's not **fair**!

Job 20:4–11,29

'The mirth of the wicked is brief, the joy of the godless lasts but a moment.' (v5)

E ven if we don't see it as an absolute, we often see that wrongdoing should be punished. People often talk about karma – what goes around comes around, what you do will come back to you. There's an expectation that justice will be done – in human terms, that is. And we feel justice has been done when we see someone paying for their wrongdoing – we can then feel that 'all's right with the world'. Justice is seen to be done, so all is well.

So how do we feel when it's not? When we see someone just getting away with something. When we gripe about it to our friends, on social media… Especially if it's something heinous. As I write this Ukraine is constantly in the news and what is happening doesn't seem fair at all. The justice that is needed for Ukraine and its people is as yet not happening. It's not fair. How can anyone get justice in this world?

This is much of what Job is dealing with. What is happening to him is not fair and nothing is being done about it in his eyes. He wouldn't be wrong in saying this. Zophar is only saying here what society expects, that wrongdoers will get their punishment.

God's take on this is different. Fairness isn't what matters. We won't be guaranteed to get what's fair according to the world. Thankfully God doesn't work according to the world's expectation. He works outside that. He sees the bigger picture, as we don't have that bigger view and can't expect to see how His justice works, and how the *timing* of that justice works. It's not according to our rules, but His. Not according to our timing, but His.

For Prayer and reflection

God, please help me see that even when it doesn't seem fair, you have a larger plan and you have it in hand. Amen.

Finding **wisdom**

'The fear of the Lord – that is wisdom, and to shun evil is understanding.' (v28)

We're looking at a portion of Job's discourse, addressing his friends in a passage that gives us a hint on wisdom. We've not read much about wisdom yet in Job, yet it's core to the book. It's not something we can find in the physical world. You can't find it in the deepest depths of the earth or the ocean, or the highest heights of the mountains or the sky. It's not available to any of the creatures that roam the earth, seas or skies. Job is realising that wisdom is not something that is easily accessible. God knows where to find it but is not giving any hint of its whereabouts or how Job should go about finding it.

So how *do* you find wisdom? Solomon was granted it when he asked God for it, and was told 'I will give you a wise and discerning heart, so that there will never have been anyone like you, nor will there ever be' (1 Kings 3:12). However, this doesn't help us in our search for wisdom. If Solomon is the only one singled out to receive wisdom this way, we can't count on this as a way of obtaining wisdom for ourselves.

But we do have a hint from Job – 'the fear of the Lord' is where to start. 'The fear of the LORD is the beginning of wisdom...' (Prov. 9:10) mirrors this almost word for word. Fear is not so much what we consider these days as being scared. It's more about having a sense of awe and reverence, a respect for the Lord and His sovereignty and divine nature. If we fear the Lord and follow His ways, that is in itself wise. And if we ask God for wisdom, He might not give it to us instantly like Solomon, but He will guide us in our search for it.

For Prayer and reflection

Lord God, we praise You for Your awesome nature and Your sovereignty. Help us to learn wisdom by following Your ways. Amen.

Lashing **out**

Job 30:20–31

'I cry out to you, God, but you do not answer...' (v20)

Even though he's learning helpful bits about wisdom, Job still gets frustrated by everything that's happening. The two are not mutually exclusive. You can be learning a lot about yourself and God, and still be frustrated about the way you're learning it. Job is being mocked, he's lost his position in society, and he's lashing out at the one who is still there.

That reminds me a little of children. As they grow, they push at their boundaries, in part to widen them as they mature, but in part to know where they will be pushed back. To know where they are safe. When they are safe, they will know where they can let out feelings and not scare that person away. Children lash out at a parent or carer knowing that doing this will not push them away. Part of the responsibility of being a parent or carer is pushing back, to show where those boundaries are. Children won't know what is OK unless they get told when it's not so.

In the same way, God will tell us when boundaries are being pushed too far. And because of that, He's safe to be with. He is big and can cope with us lashing out at Him. Have you ever been angry but fearful of what God might do if you direct your anger at Him? He understands us perfectly. He already knows what we're angry about and what's on our mind – and He knows that sometimes lashing out and venting to Him is exactly what we need. His reaction to our venting is to 'rejoice over you with gladness; he will quiet you by his love' (Zeph. 3:17, ESV), which I see as God quietening us as a toddler is quietened in the lap of their parent, soothed by lullabies and gentle shh-ing.

For Prayer and reflection

Next time you feel angry, vent to God. Express your thoughts, your feelings, your desires.

Weekend

Consider the wonders

....

Matthew 6:25–34

'See how the flowers of the field grow.' (v28)

Time for a weekend in nature. Job is told by Elihu in tomorrow's passage to 'consider God's wonders' (Job 37:14). We're looking here at a passage we've often read, but maybe haven't acted on. How often do we stop to 'consider the lilies' (Matt 6:28, ESV) beyond giving them thirty seconds' thought when we read the passage? Let's spend time in nature – but this time with the inquisitive nature of a toddler who stops to look at a ladybird on a piece of grass. No rushing this time without looking at your surroundings.

Look at the plants around you. Do they have leaves, or have they changed colour yet and begun to fall? Look at the colours and the detail, consider the seasonal cycle. Any flowers, wild or tame? Look at the detail, the mathematical arrangements of the different parts. Maybe you'll even find some fractals. On the beach? Consider the grains of sand, the details on the shells. This detail is from the God who created each piece, yet they are not so important as us, the humans He created in His own image. If He goes to that much effort for them, how much more will He do for us?

....

For Prayer and reflection

Take time to go for a walk and look for God in the amazing nature He created for us.

The **insight** of youth

Job 32:1–17

'It is not only the old who are wise, not only the aged who understand what is right.' (v9)

Elihu hasn't been mentioned before now. Younger in age than Eliphaz, Bildad and Zophar, out of respect for his elders he has waited until they finish to have his say. He gets closer to the answer than the first three friends did, but still doesn't *quite* make it to the full truth. He is, however, far more courteous to Job than the three so-called friends have been.

Elihu may be speaking from a revelation from God. Though not the one with the final answer, he helps point the way to the one with the full answer. He has lots of riches to impart – he is closer to speaking wisdom than the three friends. Elihu, in this situation, can perhaps be seen as a parallel to John the Baptist pointing the way to Jesus. Elihu was young and may not have been seen as having the experience or knowledge to be worth sharing. As Paul said to Timothy, 'Don't let anyone look down on you because you are young' (1 Tim 4:12).

Do you find yourself assuming that someone won't have the knowledge or experience you need because of their youth, or another reason? We risk overlooking someone because of their youth (or how they dress or behave) because of our biases or preconceived ideas. We may not even *realise* that we have any biases. Given a chance, we might allow an Elihu to speak, and they may speak more truthfully than an Eliphaz, a Bildad, or a Zophar. Who is in your life who might fit that description? Someone you pass on the street, someone in your church, or even in your family. It could be anyone. It's worth considering if you are showing bias, and whether this person has something important to say.

For Prayer and reflection

Lord, who do I know who is like Elihu, who has knowledge to share and isn't being heard? Help me give them space to speak Your truth. Amen.

Overwhelmed with **majesty**

'Who has the
wisdom to count
the clouds?' (v37)

Finally, we hear from God. He has been quiet for a long time, and we have heard much semi-truth from Job's so-called friends. Job has been desperate for *some* word from God to explain what has been happening to him. Maybe this is it now? Maybe we'll find out why Job was allowed to suffer, or where Job can find wisdom...

This passage reads almost like poetry, it's so pretty to read and it has such wonderful description. Yet instead of hearing answers, Job gets only questions from God: 'Does the rain have a father?... Do you know the laws of the heavens?... Who gives the ibis wisdom?' All these questions, beautiful as they are, are impossible to answer. Job can of course do none of these.

Instead, Job is overwhelmed with God's might and majesty, much as we ourselves would likely be with these questions – questions which serve as examples of God's power and sovereignty. Served with many examples of how God controls the world, Job *has* to admit humility. He has to admit that in accusing God of being unjust, he was accusing a being with wisdom and power far beyond anything he could ever imagine. What Job begins to learn is that he doesn't know as much as he thought he did. A case of the more you know, the more you realise you don't know.

Can we admit humility? When our learning reveals that the knowledge we knew was but a fraction of the total, are we ready to admit that we *don't* know much more than we *do* know? What God asks of us is to 'walk humbly with your God' (Mic. 6:8). If we take that verse to heart, we will not go wrong. Let's use the verse from Micah then, as our prayer.

**For Prayer
and reflection**

Lord, keep me
humble in my walk
with You. Your
majesty is far
above the heavens
– keep my soul
rooted in You and
my feet on the
ground. Amen.

Leviathan and Behemoth

Job 40:15–41:10

'Can you pull in Leviathan with a fishhook or tie down its tongue with a rope?' (41:1)

Behemoth and Leviathan are two humongous animals. Part of God's creation, one lives on land, the other in the sea. It's believed that Behemoth is a giant hippopotamus, and Leviathan a huge crocodile, though it is also believed that these are symbolic creatures rather than real.

They represent human nature and the world systems, with the devil behind them. Whereas God has made them, therefore has power over them, we as mere humans cannot expect to stand up to these monsters. So, if we can't stand up to human nature and the world systems, how on earth can we think we could stand up to God? And how on earth could we think we can demand that God answers our questions?

This seems to be more about our attitude behind the questioning. God has given us a right to approach him – but not a right to demand answers. We can ask him all we like, but He will answer in His own way, in His own time. He is the one with power over creation, so we must respect that. We can 'approach God's throne of grace with confidence' (Heb. 4:16) but at the same time we must respect God's might and majesty.

There is a time to approach God's throne as a child of God, but there is also a time to approach with reverence, aware of God's sovereignty over all. To go into the throne room not as if it were our living room, but as if it were the most holy of holies as in the temple in Jerusalem. We need to remember this is the God who created the whole earth and the creatures that inhabit it, the Lord who flung the stars into space and created the celestial bodies. He is worthy of reverence.

For Prayer and reflection

Lord, I'm sorry for the times I have demanded answers from You. Help me to remember that You have heard my prayers and will answer them in Your time. Amen.

Time to let go

'Surely I spoke of things I did not understand, things too wonderful for me to know.' (v3)

ob's reply to God is short. He does not waste his words – he has realised that God is God, and that is all he will know. He has a greater idea of God's majesty – and with that, a greater sense of how much he doesn't know. He is beginning to learn wisdom, as much through what has been omitted as through that which has been said. By fearing God, and not looking for wisdom where it won't be found, he has obtained some wisdom for himself.

Job finally realises that though he wants – even needs – an answer for why he has suffered, God might *never* give him what he wants. He may never know why he lost everything. Having realised this, he keeps his reply short – there is no point in wasting words.

Can we let God be the majestic all-powerful God, who doesn't owe us any explanation? This might mean letting go of things we are holding tightly and rigidly to. This may be quite a challenge.

What can help is to picture ourselves holding something in our hands. Holding the hand tightly closed around the item means we can't let it go, and if taken from us may hurt a lot. Imagine taking a sharp knife from a closed hand! If we open our hands, it won't hurt us when we let go of it. Visualising this and using these hand actions can be a great help in trying to let something go into God's hands. When we come to God with open hands, not only can we prepare to let go, but we can prepare to receive now that item is no longer in the way.

For Prayer and reflection

Lord, please help me let go of anything I'm holding too tightly. Help me let go of any expectations I will get an answer. You are the God above everything. Amen.

They all lived **happily** ever after

Job 42:7–17

'The LORD blessed the latter part of Job's life more than the former part.' (v12)

It's been a bit of a whistle-stop tour through Job, and we've only covered a portion of it! The questions you may have had at the start might not have been answered. Our wrestle for wisdom has led us mostly through where not to find it, and we've had some challenging things to think and pray about.

In the end, Job was given even more than he lost; family assets, reputation – and he lived a long life. He died without getting answers to his questions – but he knew God had been there throughout and was still Sovereign. Somehow, with his faith, nothing changed, but yet everything changed. He went to hell and back, and kept his faith all the way through, yet it was deepened, rounded out, scarred. You don't go through what Job experienced and come through unscathed or unchanged. It's like knocking down scaffolding that has been keeping your faith up, and then working out exactly what you need in place of the scaffolding to give your faith a good support.

In Genesis we read of Jacob's wrestle with an angel, where he was left with a limp (Gen. 32:22–31), a souvenir of a divine encounter. Things like this leave their mark on us. Job may have been left with scars from his sores, and perhaps other unseen scars. Your own events may have left you with scars, physical or mental. Rather than hiding those scars for fear of what others will say, we should consider they are reminders of what we have come through and what we have learned in the process. They show how far we've come. Scars mean you survived and healed. Scars are things to be proud of.

And above all, God is with us through everything.

For Prayer and reflection

Lord, thank You for those scars I have, seen or unseen. I thank You that they are a part of my story that show I made it through. Amen.

IIIII PRISONS WEEK
A WEEK OF PRAYER

At Waverley Abbey Trust we believe in helping people to love God and love all. Living that way makes a positive impact in every walk of life, and particularly in prisons. That's why we're committed to Prison Week. We want to see more of God's Kingdom sweep through the prison system.

Prisons Week equips and enables the Church to pray for all those affected by prisons: prisoners and their families, victims of crime and their communities, those working in the criminal justice system and the many people who are involved in caring for those affected by crime on the inside and outside of our prisons. Prisons Week produces resources and provides an annual focus and reason for Christians to unite together in prayer that moves the heart of God to action.

Prisons Sunday – the second Sunday in October – marks the beginning of the week of prayer each year, running through until the following Saturday.

For more information visit **wvly.org/prisons-week**

NATURALLY SUPERNATURAL

WENDY MANN

....

John 15:1–8

'If you remain in me and I in you, you will bear much fruit...' (v5)

W e're going to go on a journey together over the next month, looking at the life we're called to live as we look at Jesus' example. However, before we start, I want to make one thing really clear. Our heavenly Father promises that if we prioritise Him, if we surrender to Him, we *will* bear much fruit.

The danger as we embark on this adventure is that we try to do things in our own strength. We get vision for living like Jesus, but we forget that everything Jesus did flowed out of intimacy with His Father. The other pitfall we can experience is comparison. We look at the fruit in our lives, compare it to the fruit of others, and conclude that Jesus hasn't anointed us for a naturally supernatural life after all.

Let's start this devotional by being clear about the truth. All of us are called by God to do the stuff that Jesus did. His promise over our lives as we follow His example is that we will bear *much* fruit. Our key role on the journey is to fix our eyes on Jesus and keep falling more and more in love with Him. Let's remain in Him and see what amazing things He'll do through us.

....

Optional further reading

Wendy Mann, *Naturally Supernatural* (UK: Malcolm Down Publishing, 2015)

The **normal** Christian life

I love how Peter summarises the life of Jesus in this passage. He tells Cornelius and his household that Jesus was anointed with the Holy Spirit and power and that He went around doing good and healing all who were oppressed by the devil. Peter then finishes by telling them that Jesus was able to do all this because God was with Him.

When we look at the life of Jesus we see what the normal Christian life looks like. Everywhere Jesus went He told people about the kingdom of God and He showed them what God's kingdom looks like when it comes. He then passed the baton for this way of living to His disciples, who have now passed the baton to us. Jesus was naturally supernatural and, as His disciples, we get to follow in His footsteps.

The truth is that the same Holy Spirit who anointed Jesus now anoints us. The same God who was with Jesus, who enabled Him to heal the sick and set people free, is now with us. We have the privilege of speaking about and demonstrating God's kingdom wherever we go, and we can start by looking for opportunities to do good.

I love that Peter includes this in his summary of Jesus' life. It makes a naturally supernatural life so accessible, because all of us can do good to others. Buy someone a coffee; thank the person serving you at the checkout; say hello to the person walking past you, and then see what the Father will do. As we follow Jesus' example, the God of the universe promises to be with us. I want to encourage you to let that truth stir your faith and give you courage as you start this adventure.

Acts 10:37–48

'God anointed Jesus of Nazareth with the Holy Spirit and power…'
(v38)

For Prayer and reflection

Thank You, Jesus, for showing me the normal Christian life. Give me passion and motivation to see Your kingdom come wherever I go. I want to follow in Your footsteps. Amen.

Our **mandate**

Matthew 10:1–8

'Heal those who are ill, raise the dead, cleanse those who have leprosy, drive out demons.' (v8)

When Jesus told His disciples in Matthew 9 that the harvest is plentiful but the workers are few, He encouraged them to pray for more people to proclaim and demonstrate the kingdom. Then at the beginning of Matthew 10 the disciples became the answer to their prayers, as Jesus sent them out to do what He had been doing. Heal the sick, raise the dead, cleanse lepers and cast out demons was their mandate. This is our mandate too.

The first time I saw someone healed I was doing an Alpha course. During one of the evenings the guy leading said He felt that God wanted to heal someone's ear. A man put his hand up to indicate that he had ear pain, and we all watched intently as he was prayed for. The prayer was short and simple and the man was quickly asked if he could feel any difference. I remember him looking surprised and touching his ear. All the pain had gone. Jesus had healed him in front of our eyes.

Jesus loves to use ordinary people to do extraordinary things. I have seen many people healed since that Alpha evening. I have also discovered that the harvest really is plentiful. So many people around us are longing for love and acceptance that can only be found in Christ. We have the joy of pointing them to Jesus through our kind words, actions and prayers.

There's no pressure on us to make things happen. Without Jesus we can do nothing. He's the only one who can save and heal. As we go around doing good He loves to give us all we need to fulfil our mandate. As we freely receive from Him, we're able to freely give away to others. *With* Jesus, anything is possible.

For Prayer and reflection

Look for opportunities to do good to others today and see if God opens the door for conversations or prayer.

Moved with **compassion**

Jesus was regularly moved with compassion. His encounter with these blind men is just one example from the gospels. Jesus' love for people motivated Him to respond to their needs and reveal the kingdom. Love must be our motivation too.

I used to speak to people about Jesus and offer to pray for them because I thought that's what made me a good Christian, and when I didn't do it I would feel bad. Then when I started to see people healed it made me feel validated in my walk with God. I tried to live a naturally supernatural life because it made me feel better about myself. Thankfully Jesus gently convicted me and my heart began to change.

The truth is that telling people about Jesus and showing them what He's like is not about us. It doesn't make God love us any more when we pray for the sick, and we don't get any brownie points when we go around doing good. The only reason we're able to do the stuff that Jesus did is because of God's grace, and the motivation for us living this way must be love for the person in front of us. Jesus has so much love in His heart for the people we meet. Our job is to show them, in a very small way, just how loved they are.

Thankfully our ability to love well is not dependent on us. In 1 John 4:19 we read that, 'We love because he first loved us.' In order to grow in love and compassion for others, we start by asking God to reveal more of His love and compassion for us. The more we grasp how loved we are, the more we will be moved with compassion to meet people's needs and bring God's kingdom wherever we go.

Matthew 20:29–34

'Jesus had compassion on them and touched their eyes.' (v34)

For Prayer and reflection

Father, would You fill me with the love and compassion You have for me, so that I can give this away to the people around me. I want to be moved with compassion. Amen.

Kindness leads to repentance

'I will pay back four times the amount.' (v8)

O f all the people Jesus could have stayed and spent time with, Zacchaeus was an unexpected choice. As a tax collector, Zacchaeus was despised by the people. Yet, Jesus made a beeline for him in the crowd in order to spend time with him. The result of Jesus' kindness was a transformed life. Zacchaeus was so impacted that he promised to give people back *four times* the amount he'd stolen.

Jesus shows kindness to everyone, but I think He has a particular soft spot for those rejected by society. I wonder if that's because these people aren't expecting to be noticed or don't feel worthy of love in the first place. When we follow in Jesus' footsteps and show kindness to those who have been ostracised, we have the privilege of seeing God's kingdom come.

I remember when some friends and I started to connect with a guy on the streets. Over several weeks we bought him lunch and spent time getting to know him. As we showed him kindness and spoke to him about Jesus, it wasn't long before he realised his need of forgiveness and invited Jesus into his life. It was incredible to see the joy in this man's eyes as he spoke about God's unconditional acceptance of him.

Kindness is a powerful tool in a naturally supernatural life. When we're kind to the people around us, especially those whom society has rejected, we give them a glimpse of what God is like. And when people see God and realise He's picked them out of the crowd to spend time with them, there is so much potential for lives to be changed. God's kindness leads people to repentance.

For Prayer and reflection

Father, would You open my eyes today to see those rejected by society. Help me to see them as You see them and to show them a glimpse of Your kindness. Amen.

Do you **know** the Father?

John 14:1–14

'Anyone who has
seen me has seen
the Father.' (v9)

get a lot of comfort from the disciples' repeated lack of understanding of what Jesus is trying to teach them. In this scripture Jesus is speaking about His Father and Philip pipes up about not knowing who the Father is. I think Jesus must have done the first-century equivalent of today's face palm. He reiterated to the disciples that He and the Father are one and that because they knew Him, they knew the Father.

The truth is that Jesus came to reveal and bring us back into relationship with the Father. The ultimate goal of the cross was not that our sins could be forgiven. The ultimate goal of the cross was that a perfect heavenly Father could adopt us as dearly loved sons and daughters. Knowing God as our Father, not just as head knowledge but through revelation from the Holy Spirit, is key if we want to live a naturally supernatural life.

When we know God as our Father it gives us greater faith and expectation when we pray, because we know the things He loves to do and what He is capable of. Knowing God as our Father also gives us greater courage to take risks in extending His kingdom, because we know that His love for us is nothing to do with our performance. Knowing God, not just as a Father 'out there', but as a Father **to us** changes everything. The great news is that God has chosen to reveal His Father heart to us through His son, Jesus.

Like the disciples, there is so much for us to learn and enjoy about God as our Father. I want to encourage you to go on a journey of discovering more about who He is by looking at Jesus. Anyone who has seen Him has seen the Father.

**For Prayer
and reflection**

**Spend some time
looking at Jesus in
the Gospels and
ask the Holy Spirit
to show you what
the Father is like.
Write down what
He reveals to you.**

Weekend

Do you know who you are?

....

Mark 1:9–11

'You are my Son, whom I love; with you I am well pleased.' (v11)

I love this moment in Scripture. Right at the start of Jesus' ministry He has this wonderful connection with His Father. The Father tears open heaven to declare His affirmation over His Son. He tells Jesus that He loves Him and is well pleased with Him, and this is before Jesus had done anything of significance ministry wise. This interaction has huge implications for us.

The instant we said yes to Jesus and chose to follow Him we were given brand-new identities. We were adopted as dearly loved sons and daughters, with the God of the universe as our Father. In addition to this, Scripture is packed full of other incredible truths of who we now are because of the cross. We have been transformed!

Everything the Bible says about us is all because of God's grace. None of us deserve it and we can do nothing to earn it. The Father declares His affirmation over us before we do anything of significance ministry wise. This means we can pursue a naturally supernatural life knowing that, no matter what happens, our Father in heaven is well pleased with us.

Do you know who you are?

....

Optional further reading

Eric B. Johnson, *Christ in You* (USA: Chosen Books, 2015)

WAVERLEY ABBEY
COLLEGE

Introduction to Christian Care & Counselling

Designed for anyone who wants to learn about themselves and how to help others effectively

You'll cover topics including:

- The biblical basis for care and counselling
- Reason and causes for problems
- Developing basic counselling skills

Farnham campus
31st Oct - 4th Nov 2022

Bradford campus
(One day a week)
Sat - Nov 5, 12, 19, 26
Dec 3 2022

wvly.org/iccc

A work of the **Spirit**

Romans 8:14–17

'The Spirit himself testifies with our spirit that we are God's children.' (v16)

Paul's focus in these verses is our adoption. We are now sons and daughters of God and He is our Father. Paul also underlines the crucial role that the Holy Spirit plays in helping us live in this truth. It's the Holy Spirit who brings about our adoption, who enables us to connect to God as a Father, and who reveals to us that we are children. Living in this truth is a work of the Spirit.

Before I did an Alpha Course I didn't understand who the Holy Spirit was or what He did. In fact, I used to be scared of Him when I saw Him meeting with people in church. During Alpha I learnt more about the Holy Spirit and then I had the opportunity to be filled with Him one evening. It was a beautiful moment.

I remember feeling warmth flood through my body as I experienced God's love in a way I'd never known before. It felt like God had come close all of a sudden and I remember crying for ages because I felt so overwhelmed. The Holy Spirit had woken something up in my heart, which had been asleep up to that point.

Since that first encounter with the Holy Spirit I have met with Him many, many times and I have learnt, first-hand, the truth of Romans 8. The Holy Spirit has shown me who God is as my Father and who I am as His daughter, and He wants to show you these truths too.

Knowing God as our Father and knowing who we are as dearly loved children is crucial if we want to live naturally supernatural lives. I want to encourage you to ask the Holy Spirit to show you the truth. All of us need His help and He is eager to come. Growing in this revelation is a work of the Spirit.

For Prayer and reflection

Holy Spirit of adoption, please would you come and fill me afresh. Give me greater revelation of who God is as my Father and who I am as His dearly loved child. Amen.

You will receive **power**

Acts 1:1–8

'But you will
receive power
when the Holy
Spirit comes on
you...' (v8)

I t was really important to Jesus that His disciples
didn't do anything until they had received the
promised Holy Spirit. We have already seen that
the Holy Spirit is key in revealing to us the truth about
who God is and who we are. The Holy Spirit is also the
one who gives us power to be witnesses and see God's
kingdom come through us wherever we go.

Sometimes I look at my life and at this scripture and
I wonder if I've actually been baptised in the Holy Spirit.
Jesus told His disciples they would receive power when
the Holy Spirit came upon them. I have definitely seen
a measure of power as I've seen people healed and set
free as I've prayed, but I am longing for so much more.
We need more awe and wonder of God in the Church
and on the streets. People grow in awe and wonder
when they see God do what only He can do, when
they see His power on display. How are your awe and
wonder levels?

Living a naturally supernatural life involves seeing
God's power flow through you, so that impossible
situations bow the knee to His superiority. The truth
is that we're completely dependent on God to see His
power in our lives. Without Him we can do nothing, but
with Him anything is possible. Our role is to submit, ask,
trust and obey. He is the only one who can heal, set free
and save.

Just in case you're tempted to disqualify yourself from
being used to bring His power, the truth is that God's
power is made perfect in our weakness (2 Cor. 12:9).
Jesus says the Holy Spirit will give us power. Let's take
God at His word, ask Him for more and pursue awe and
wonder moments so that Jesus is glorified.

**For Prayer
and reflection**

Take some time to
reflect on
moments in your
life that have
caused you to be
in awe and wonder
of God. Let this
exercise stir your
faith and prayers
for more.

Reveal the **Father**

John 20:19–23

'As the Father has sent me, I am sending you.' (v21)

Jesus has risen from the dead and has come to reveal Himself to His disciples. What we see in this scripture is a commissioning moment. Jesus breathes on His disciples so that they are filled with the Holy Spirit. He then gives them this beautiful mandate, 'As the Father has sent me, I am sending you.' (v21). How had the Father sent Jesus? As a dearly loved Son, full of the power of the Spirit, to reveal the Father wherever He went. We are now sent in the same way.

Our main motivation in living a naturally supernatural life should be to show people what the Father is like and give them a glimpse of His heart. When we are kind to people and look for opportunities to do good, we show people the Father. When we accept and love those whom society rejects and we forgive people who have wronged us, we show people the Father. When we pray for people to be healed and we share prophetic words with people, we give them a glimpse of what the Father is like.

The truth is that there is a desperate need for people across our planet to meet the Father heart of God. Fatherlessness is rife in our world and societies are suffering the consequences of people starved of a father's affirmation and love. The problem is vast and could easily feel overwhelming, but we serve a God for whom nothing is impossible. He is a Father to the fatherless and He's committed to revealing His love through believers like you and me.

Ask the Holy Spirit to give you more revelation of who the Father is. Then look for opportunities to share God's love with those around you. Let's be those who reveal the Father wherever we go.

For Prayer and reflection

Father, would You help me to show people what You're like wherever I go. Thank You that You are a Father to the fatherless. Amen.

Your **words** have power

Matthew 26:6–13

'Why are you bothering this woman? She has done a beautiful thing to me.' (v10)

Just imagine for a minute a different ending to this story. Imagine that Jesus didn't challenge His disciples and stick up for this woman. Imagine the negative impact on the woman's life, if the words she had ringing in her ears as she fled the scene were from the disciples. She would have left full of shame and with a wounded heart. Our words are powerful.

Thank goodness Jesus did speak up. His words celebrated the woman and what she had done. As a result, she left His presence affirmed and encouraged. I like to think that Jesus' words stayed with this woman and impacted her for the rest of her life. I'm sure she would never be the same again. Our words are powerful.

I used to be a bully when I was at school, not physically but verbally. I have seen first-hand the destructive power of harsh and unkind words. As a transformed follower of Jesus, I have also witnessed the life-giving and empowering impact of encouragement. I have seen people start to believe in themselves as I have told them what I see in them. I have seen people literally stand taller as I have spoken truth to them. I have also seen people get a glimpse of a God in heaven who loves them, as I have valued them and championed them. Our words are powerful.

It costs us very little to encourage the people around us; to tap into God's heart for them and let them know what He sees. Never underestimate the impact of a kind word, spoken or written at the right time. Our words have the potential to give a better ending to people's stories. Let's be like Jesus. Let's change people's lives with our words.

For Prayer and reflection

Jesus, thank You for showing me how powerful my words are. Help me to be known as an encourager and to use my words to reveal Your love to the people around me. Amen.

Be **eager** to prophesy

1 Corinthians 14:1–4

'Follow the way of love and eagerly desire gifts of the Spirit, especially prophecy.' (v1)

The Holy Spirit loves to give us gifts. In this passage Paul specifically talks about the gifts of tongues and prophesy. He tells us that when we speak in tongues we strengthen ourselves, but when we prophesy we comfort, strengthen and encourage others. This is true when we prophesy in the church. It's also true when we prophesy over those who don't yet know Jesus.

Prophecy is an extension of encouragement. When we prophesy we get to share with people what God thinks and feels about them. Hearing God's voice is something every Christian can do, but how I hear Him will be different to how you hear Him. We learn how He speaks to us as we spend time with Him and practise sharing what we think He says.

I remember when I prophesied over a lady and her daughter in a coffee shop. The thoughts I had from God were very vague and I could easily have dismissed them. Yet, when I tentatively shared them, I realised that God was speaking and the women were really encouraged. God saw them and knew what they needed to hear, and I had the privilege of sharing His heart that day. Both of them ended up coming to church as a result of our conversation.

For Prayer and reflection

Ask God what He wants to say to someone that you know you're going to see today. Have a go at sharing what you think He says and see what God does.

Hearing God's voice is easy, but it takes practise and courage to prophesy. You can't know if what you think God's saying is accurate, unless you share what you've heard. I've got things wrong many times, but God has been so faithful as I've kept taking risks. God wants to speak to you for the people around you, to encourage them and show them His heart. Eagerly desire spiritual gifts, but especially that you would prophesy. Remember that your words have power.

Weekend

Do you talk about Jesus?

. . . .

Acts 2:22–39

'When the people heard this, they were cut to the heart...' (v37)

I love Peter's boldness in this passage. He went from denying Jesus to confidently speaking about Him. Being filled with the Holy Spirit at Pentecost transformed Peter and gave Him great courage. His bold declaration about Jesus led to many being convicted of their sin and asking how they could be saved.

When I first started praying for people on the streets, I was so full of fear that I never stayed around long enough to ask them if God had done anything. I certainly wouldn't stick around to talk to them about Jesus. Over the years I've learnt how to more naturally bring Jesus into conversations. Asking questions like, 'Do you know Jesus?' or, 'Would you like to know Jesus?' or sharing some of your story, are great places to start as we look to make Him famous on the earth.

I still feel fear when God gives me these opportunities and I have to make a conscious decision to choose courage. The truth is that, like Peter, we all need the Holy Spirit's help to be bold. Let's ask Him to give us the courage we need to talk about Jesus more. The fields are ripe for harvest.

. . . .

Optional further reading

Claire Coggan, *Go: Everyday Stories of Stopping to Love* (UK: Malcolm Down Publishing, 2020)

Seek **first** the kingdom

**Matthew
6:25–34**

'But seek first his kingdom and his righteousness…'
(v33)

Jesus is talking about worry, something we all wrestle with in our lives. In other translations the word 'anxiety' is used. There is so much anxiety in the world and the Church today. Here Jesus gives us the antidote.

Jesus' is specifically targeting anxiety around our basic need for food and clothing, but we can apply what He teaches to any area of need we have. The core of Jesus' message is clear: we don't need to worry or be anxious about *anything* because He knows what we need and He *loves* to provide.

Instead of worrying, Jesus instructs us to seek first His kingdom. As disciples of Jesus we're called to prioritise Him and His way of living. We're called to put Him first and pursue a supernatural life, which points to Him and gives Him glory. With so many things competing for our attention and so much we could worry about, Jesus instructs us to focus our energy on just one thing. Seek first God's kingdom. He'll take care of everything else.

This is Jesus' antidote to anxiety, and it makes a lot of sense when you think about it. In order to seek first God's kingdom, we have to take our eyes off our circumstances and ourselves and we have to fix our eyes on Him. When we fix our eyes on Him, we remember who He is and what He's capable of, and faith rises as a result. It's very difficult for faith and worry to co-exist.

We have the incredible privilege of being drafted into God's mission on the earth. Let's fix our eyes on the King and prioritise His kingdom. As we do, we can be confident that He knows what we need and He loves to provide. He is a good Father and we can trust Him.

For Prayer and reflection

Thank You, Father, for Your generous provision in my life. Help me to be someone who prioritises your kingdom. I want to be free from worry as I keep my eyes fixed on You. Amen.

Give to make a difference

Our Bible reading notes are read by hundreds of thousands of people around the world. *Every Day with Jesus* and *Inspiring Women Every Day* are now free in the UK. We want everyone, whatever their financial means to have access to these resources that help them walk each day with our Saviour.

It makes all the difference. One reader in Malaysia said:

When I was first exposed Every Day with Jesus about two years ago, I could sense something different, something refreshing, and I was energised. I used to struggle to translate knowledge into my daily life. EDWJ helped me to be more insightful, more positive, and to enjoy everyday life as a disciple. This helps me to be patient and positive at home, at work, and at church.

As we trust in God's provision, we know there are costs to providing this ministry. Can you give to make a difference in someone's life? Could supporting this vision be a way in which you serve?

A gift of just £2 a month from you will put daily Bible reading notes into the hands of at least one person who is hungry to know God and experience His presence every day.

Visit **wvly.org/donate** to give to make a difference, or use the form at the back of these notes.

Fall in love with the **King**

Matthew 22:34–40

'Love the Lord your God with all your heart and with all your soul and with all your mind.' (v37)

One of the main ways we'll be motivated to seek first God's kingdom, is to increasingly fall in love with the King. Jesus showed us what prioritising God's kingdom means. Everywhere He went He told people about the kingdom and then He demonstrated what it looks like. Jesus is our example. The more we fall in love with Him, the more what's important to Jesus will become important to us.

Our motivation for seeing God's kingdom come has to be love for Jesus. Living like Jesus takes courage and requires us to surrender to God's plan for our lives. If we reach out to people because we think that's what being a good Christian looks like, the people we speak to will feel like projects and we'll be tempted to give up when we don't see the breakthrough we long for. But, if we reach out to people because we love God with every fibre of our being and we want to honour Him and show His love to others, we will be motivated to be naturally supernatural over the long haul.

How are you doing at loving God with all your heart, soul and mind? Has He got first place in your life? I think it can be easy to say we love God, but then live in a way that means we hold things back from Him. Following Jesus is a life-long journey of surrendering to Him, and then surrendering again. It's about being all in and loving Him with all that we are. When we start with loving Jesus, we are increasingly able to receive His love for us, which in turn enables us to love the people around us. When Jesus is at the centre of your life, you will lack nothing and the kingdom that's important to Him will become important to you.

For Prayer and reflection

Jesus, I'm sorry for the parts of my heart that I hold back from You. Help me to fall more in love with You, so that what's important to You becomes important to me. Amen.

He is **able**

Mark 9:14–29

'Everything is possible for one who believes.' (v23)

There are two questions that people often ask, either consciously or unconsciously, when it comes to seeing God's kingdom come in power. Is God really able to transform lives and does He actually want to? We'll answer the second question in tomorrow's devotional. Today's passage shows us the answer to the first.

The disciples can't help this little boy and his father is desperate. When Jesus comes along, He asks the father a few questions and then the father reveals the unbelief lurking in his heart. 'If you can do anything, please help us.' The father is asking what many of us ask in our hearts but maybe don't verbalise with our mouths, 'Are you really able to change lives, Jesus?' 'Can you really heal that?' 'Is there really hope for that situation?' 'Can that person actually be free?'

These questions aren't wrong to ask. The alternative is that we keep them buried in an attempt to hide our wrestles with faith. The problem with this approach is that the questions don't get dealt with and neither does our unbelief. When we verbalise our questions and doubts, Jesus is able to rush in with the truth. 'Everything is possible for one who believes.' Then, like the father, we can ask Jesus to help us believe.

The truth is that Jesus has all power and all authority. He defeated the enemy on the cross and now sits in a place of complete and utter victory. *Nothing* is impossible for Him, which means *nothing* is impossible for us. Jesus answers our first question loud and clear in this passage. He really can transform any life. We do believe God. Help us overcome our unbelief.

For Prayer and reflection

Think about someone you know who seems least likely to give their life to Jesus. As you pray for them, reflect on the truth that Jesus is able to transform anyone.

He is **willing**

Matthew 8:1–4

"'I am willing," he said. "Be clean!'"
(v3)

The man in this story didn't question Jesus' ability to heal him. He knew that Jesus could deal with his leprosy in an instant. The question in this man's heart was different. Did Jesus actually *want* to heal him? Jesus' answer came loud and clear again, 'I *am* willing... Be clean.'

Over the years I have wrestled with this question and the one we considered yesterday. I have wondered about God's ability to bring breakthrough and I have questioned His willingness to move in response to my prayers. If I'm honest, the question about His willingness to heal has been a particular battle. I have struggled with various health issues for a lot of my life. When I had to have a hysterectomy at the age of forty-one, with a deep longing to be a mum and no kids, there was a lot of grief in my heart to process. There is no quick fix for this kind of journey.

Yet, in the midst of my pain and mystery, and yours, the truth remains the same.

Jesus is able to do anything *and* He wants to break in and heal. Jesus is willing. This is the truth that the leper's interaction with Jesus teaches us, and we have to hold onto it if we want to do what Jesus did.

Despite my own battles with sickness, I have prayed with countless others for healing and seen God move miraculously. Knowing that God is willing to heal is what motivates me to keep asking. There's nothing quite like the look on someone's face when Jesus heals them. Praying for the sick is an immense privilege that all of us are called to. Have you settled in your heart that God is willing to heal? I want to encourage you to reflect on and receive this truth afresh today.

For Prayer and reflection

Thank You, Jesus, that You love to heal. Please put this truth deep in my heart so that I am motivated to keep praying for myself and others. Amen.

He loves **faith**

I love seeing Jesus interacting with women in the Bible. In this story we get to see Jesus' power to heal and His kindness and compassion towards the marginalised. We also get to see the incredible faith of a woman who had been sick for many years, but who never gave up hope for her healing.

The scripture tells us that this woman had been sick for twelve years and that she had spent all her money trying to find a cure. Nothing had worked, but when she saw Jesus walking by, hope rose in her heart again, 'If I can just touch His cloak.'

I find this woman's faith so inspiring. If I'd been in her shoes I think I would have given up hope years earlier and, instead, worked out a way to cope with my sickness. This woman kept faith alive in her heart and Jesus honoured her for it.

Jesus loves faith. He loves it when we believe and pray for things that are impossible without Him. He celebrates us when we put ourselves in positions that require courage, like the woman pushing through the crowd. Our faith pleases God's heart. The great news is that we only need faith as small as a mustard seed to move mountains. Everything is possible for those who believe. The sobering news is that the enemy hates our faith and will do all that he can to smother it. We must be intentional about guarding and growing the faith in our hearts so that we can keep hope alive and believe for more.

Over the next few days we'll look at how we can add fuel to the faith in our hearts. Living a naturally supernatural life requires faith. With the smallest amount we can see God's kingdom come in staggering ways.

Mark 5:21–34

'Daughter, your faith has healed you. Go in peace and be freed from your suffering.' (v34)

For Prayer and reflection

Thank You, Jesus, for the example of the woman in this story. Help me to be more like her when it comes to faith and hope in my heart. Amen.

Weekend

Do you struggle with mystery?

....

Psalm 13:1–6

'But I trust in your unfailing love…' (v5)

I love the Psalms. They often show us people's raw emotion in the midst of mystery. In this Psalm David starts by expressing his frustration to God about the situation he's in. By the end of the Psalm, David is in a different place. He's declaring his trust in God. He's come back to a place of worship.

There's a lot of mystery to navigate when you pursue a naturally supernatural life. There will be times when you don't see the breakthrough you're praying for.

Sometimes you'll pluck up courage to take a big risk and it will seem like God is silent. When we seek first the kingdom we'll see many amazing miracles. We'll also have to learn to navigate mystery well.

The Psalms teach us how to do that. We need to get gut level honest with God about how we feel about the situation we're in, without filtering what we say. Only after we've poured out our hearts do we come back to the place of worship, of declaring our trust in God. Unprocessed pain will attack our faith, but navigating mystery well will enable us to keep hope alive in our hearts. Do you need to write a psalm?

....

Optional further reading

Mark Vroegop, *Dark Clouds, Deep Mercy* (USA: Crossway, 2019)

Come like a **child**

Mark 10:13–16

'Anyone who will not receive the kingdom of God like a little child will never enter it.'
(v15)

f you want to be someone who lives a naturally supernatural life, you have to be childlike. In this scripture the disciples try to turn the children away. They see them as a distraction from the important ministry Jesus is doing, but Jesus sees them differently. Jesus sees the children as an example to us of how to live.

I have learnt so much from children over the years. They have taught me what it looks like to really trust, to live with faith, to forgive quickly, to be brave and to be full of joy. I remember being so provoked when I heard a story about a five-year-old boy who had been unwell. His mum had prayed for him to be healed but nothing had happened. The mum was about to carry on with her day when her son told her that she was to keep praying. This boy was so convinced that God wanted to heal him that his natural conclusion was for his mum to keep praying until he was healed. What beautiful childlike faith.

How are you doing at receiving God's kingdom like a child? In order to become more childlike we have to go on a continual journey of repentance. We have to identify where our thinking has become cynical, doubting or critical and ask Jesus to forgive us. Then we need to intentionally renew our minds with the truth until our thinking and behaviour changes. If we go on this journey we will be able to trust God more completely and believe Him more wholeheartedly. As a result, His kingdom will flow more freely though us.

Children can teach us so much about following Jesus if we choose to open our hearts to learn from them. Which children could you learn from today?

For Prayer and reflection

Thank You, Jesus, for the many things children can teach me about following You. Please help me to open my heart to learn so that I can grow in trust and faith. Amen.

Celebrate breakthrough

Luke 15:11–24

'Bring the fattened calf and kill it. Let's have a feast and celebrate.'
(v23)

I love this parable for so many reasons, but one of the things that really stands out to me is the way the father celebrates when his son comes home. The father's response to his son's homecoming is to give gifts and throw a lavish party. We can learn a lot about God from this moment. We have a heavenly Father who really celebrates breakthrough. The question for us is, do we do the same?

I learnt early on the importance of thanksgiving and celebration in response to God's kingdom coming. There was a time when I used to see backs healed all the time when I prayed. It was amazing but it also got boring fairly quickly. I wanted to 'progress' to seeing other, more exciting conditions healed, so I stopped celebrating and being thankful for what God was doing. Unsurprisingly the miracles soon started to dry up.

What I realised was that the miracles had become about me and my 'success' as a Christian, rather than about the person in front of me who was now pain free. The truth is that every time God meets with someone and heals them it's *incredible*. Every time God sets someone free when we pray, or draws someone to Jesus when we share the gospel, is evidence of His amazing grace. All these things should evoke an outpouring of thanksgiving and celebration from our hearts.

When we're thankful and we choose to intentionally celebrate, faith rises in our hearts because our eyes are lifted to Jesus. When we see Jesus more clearly we can't help but believe Him for more. How are you doing at really celebrating what Jesus is doing in and through you? We have so much to be thankful for.

For Prayer and reflection

Take some time to make a list of things you're thankful for and celebrating today. Use your list to stir faith in your heart to pray for more.

Remember, **remember**

Mark 8:1–9

'About this time another large crowd had gathered, and the people ran out of food again.' (v1, NLT)

The disciples find themselves in a familiar position. There's a large crowd with no food. When Jesus suggests they deal with the issue, they panic. How would they find enough food in such a remote place? It's amazing to me that the disciples had already forgotten what Jesus is able to do with a few loaves and fish. Just a few chapters earlier, Jesus involved the disciples in an incredible food-multiplying miracle with an even bigger crowd. They had seemingly not remembered what was possible for God and fear gripped their hearts.

Before we judge the disciples too harshly, we should be mindful of the fact that we're often not too different from them. How many times have we felt fear when we've needed financial provision, even though we've known God providing for us in the past? Or how often has panic set in when we're waiting for test results from the doctor, even though God has proved Himself faithful to us in all circumstances, over and over again? Just like the disciples, we are prone to forgetting what God's like and what He's capable of.

When living a naturally supernatural life, remembering is key to fixing our eyes on Jesus and stirring faith in our hearts. It's easy to think you'll never forget the people you see healed, or the opportunities you get to reveal Jesus to people. The truth is you will forget, unless you intentionally make a plan to remember. Write down how God uses you. Keep a note on your phone that you can refer to and re-read often. Remembering who God is and what He does lifts our eyes and adds fuel to our faith. When we remember we tend to be more thankful too.

For Prayer and reflection

Start a note on your phone or a page in your journal for remembering. Write down how you've seen God move through you so far and take time to celebrate.

The harvest **is** plentiful

Matthew 9:35–38

'The harvest is plentiful but the workers are few.' (v37)

Just before Jesus sent His disciples out to do what He'd been doing, He made this declaration. The harvest is plentiful, but the workers are few. Jesus then instructed His disciples to pray for more workers to be sent into the harvest. You and I get to be part of the answer to those prayers as we pursue naturally supernatural lives. In this devotional I want to home in on the abundant harvest. Grasping this truth will open our eyes and stir our faith.

Jesus told His disciples that the harvest was plentiful, that there were many people ready to respond to Him. It's my conviction that the same is true today. In a world where everything feels like it's being shaken, people are hungry for something they can really rely on. The things people used to look to and lean on for security and hope have faltered. There is only one who will remain trustworthy and true when everything else falls away. We are alive at such an opportune time to see many open up to and receive God's love.

For Prayer and reflection

Thank You, Father, for the truth that there is an abundant harvest around me. Please open my eyes to see the world through that kingdom lens. You are mighty to save. Amen.

The challenge for us is to change the way we think. If we read the news or look at what's going on around us, without the backdrop of Scripture, we will easily be discouraged and have little expectation that God's kingdom is having an impact. If, however, we lift our eyes and see everything through the kingdom lens of an abundant harvest, suddenly everything looks different.

Paul encouraged the church in Colossae to set their minds on things above, not on earthly things (Col. 3:2). We need to do the same. There are many people ready to know Jesus. The harvest is plentiful. Are you ready to go?

Next Issue

November

BRUTALLY HONEST PRAYERS OF THE BIBLE

TANYA MARLOW

December

TREASURE IN THE DARKNESS

KATY CANTY

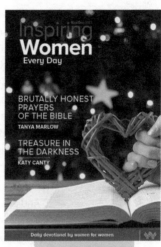

Available in a variety of formats

In **November**, Tanya Marlow will guide us through prayers recorded in Scriptures that don't hold back in their raw emotion and openness, showing us how we can gain freedom in prayer.

In **December**, as we move through Advent and Christmas, retired prison chaplain Katy Canty uses her own experiences to show how even in the most trying places and times, God is able to work deeply and we can experience Him in new and enriching ways.

Obtain your copy from waverleyabbeyresources.org

Scatter seeds

Matthew 13:1–9

'A farmer went out to sow his seed.' (v3)

The farmer in this parable was very generous with his seed scattering. He didn't brush the seed that fell on the path onto the good soil. He also didn't cut away the thorns that grew up to choke the plants that did initially take root. The farmer scattered seed everywhere. Lots of it didn't produce lasting fruit, but the seed that did produced an abundant harvest.

The truth is that as we scatter the seed of God's kingdom, lots of it won't land on good soil and it won't take root. As we share God's love with people, as we offer to pray for them, as we go around doing good, not everyone's heart will be ready to receive and that's OK. In fact, it's to be expected. God's encouragement to us through this parable is loud and clear. If we sow seed that doesn't produce fruit we shouldn't be discouraged. Not all the seed we scatter is going to grow.

And yet, as the farmer continued to generously sow his seed, some fell on good soil and what resulted was a multiplied harvest. The truth is, although not all our seed will fall on good soil, some of it will. Some of the people we offer to pray for and do good to will be really ready to receive. Their hearts will be like good soil and the result will be a multiplied harvest and an abundance of fruit. Lives will be changed, hearts will be healed and families will be impacted. You always get more than you bargained for when seed takes root in the kingdom.

Only Jesus can know if people's hearts are ready to receive. Our job is to keep generously scattering seed wherever we go. It's only a matter of time before some of it lands on good soil.

For Prayer and reflection

Thank You, Father, for the privilege of being called to sow seeds of Your kingdom wherever I go. Help me to be generous in how and where I scatter Your truth today. Amen.

Weekend

Do you know people of peace?

....

John 6:35–44

'No one can come to me unless the Father who sent me draws them…' (v44)

The harvest is plentiful and we're encouraged to be generous with the kingdom seed we sow, and yet God is the only one who can transform a person's life and bring them into His family.

I used to live under an unhealthy pressure of needing to change people and see them come to know Jesus. The above verse has really helped to lift that off and give me a new sense of freedom and joy in living a naturally supernatural life.

No one can come to Jesus unless the Father draws them. I can't draw them and neither can you. Only God can draw people to His Son. I find that truth so liberating. As I scatter seed and I go around doing good, I do so as a 'finder'. I am on the look out for the people I meet who the Father is already drawing to Christ. Those are the people whose hearts will have good soil; those are the people the Bible refers to as people of peace.

So, as you go, be a finder. Scatter loads of seed and ask the Father to lead you to the people He's already drawing. There's no pressure on you. He's the only one who can change a person's heart and He's really good at it too.

Pray and **never** give up

Luke 18:1–8

'Jesus told his disciples a parable to show them that they should always pray and not give up.' (v1)

W e don't know how much of God's kingdom we can have this side of heaven. We don't know how many miracles we'll see or how many people we'll see saved. Jesus doesn't tell us. What He does tell us though is to pray and keep praying. Jesus teaches us through this parable to pray and never give up. He also teaches us that, unlike the unjust judge, He's eager to hear our prayers and answer them.

Our prayers reveal what's going on in our hearts and the level of expectation we live with. If we have faith that God loves to heal, we'll pray for people to be healed. If we have faith that God is mighty to save, we'll keep asking God to break in with salvation. I've had different seasons over the years of really believing God for breakthrough and seasons when I've stopped praying because of disappointment. If you can relate to my journey, receive faith from this parable. Don't give up Pray and keep praying.

The truth is that our prayers are powerful and effective. It's also true that we're completely dependent on God if we want to see His kingdom come through us. He's the one who heals and only He can draw people to Jesus. Our job is to come to our Father, ask Him for big things and keep asking. Then, as we look for opportunities to go around doing good, we can trust that God will lead us to people of peace whose hearts are ready to receive.

We don't know how much of God's kingdom we can have this side of heaven, but we do know it's so much more than we currently see. As we pursue naturally supernatural lives, let's come to the Father with bold prayers. He is eager to hear and willing to respond.

For Prayer and reflection

Thank You, Father, that my prayers are powerful and effective. Help me pray bold prayers for your kingdom as I step into the supernatural life you've called me to. Amen.

Notes

**Heartbreak, Hope
and Holy Moments**

**Living with Cancer -
Walking with God**

Order form

Get Your **FREE** Daily Bible Reading Notes **TODAY!** (UK ONLY)

Your favourite Bible reading notes are now FREE. God has called us back to the original vision of CWR to provide these notes to everyone who needs them, regardless of their circumstance or ability to pay. It is our desire to see these daily Bible reading notes used more widely, to see Christians grow in their relationship with Jesus on a daily basis and to see Him reflected in their everyday living. Clearly there are costs to provide this ministry and we are trusting in God's provision.

Could you be part of this vision? Do you have the desire to see lives transformed through a relationship with Jesus? **A small donation from you of just £2 a month, by direct debit, will make such a difference** Giving hope to someone in desperate need whilst you too grow deeper in your own relationship with Jesus.

4 Easy Ways To Order

1. Visit our online store at **waverleyabbeyresources.org/store**
2. Send this form together with your payment to: **Waverley Abbey Trust, Waverley Abbey House, Waverley Lane, Farnham, Surrey GU9 8EP**
3. Phone in your credit card order: **01252 784700** (Mon–Fri, 9.30am – 4.30pm)
4. Visit a Christian bookshop

For a list of our National Distributors, who supply countries outside the UK, visit waverleyabbeyresources.org/distributors

Your Details (required for orders and donations)

Full Name: ID No. (if known):

Home Address:

                                                    Postcode:

Telephone No. (for queries):   Email:

Publications

TITLE	QTY	PRICE	TOTAL
	TOTAL PUBLICATIONS		

UK P&P: up to £24.99 = **£2.99**; £25.00 and over = **FREE**

Elsewhere P&P: up to £10 = **£4.95**; £10.01 – £50 = **£6.95**; £50.01 – £99.99 = **£10**; £100 and over = **£30**

Total Publications and P&P (please allow 14 days for delivery)   **A**

Payment Details

☐ I enclose a cheque made payable to CWR for the amount of: £ _____

☐ Please charge my credit/debit card.

Cardholder's Name (in BLOCK CAPITALS) _____

Card No. ⬚⬚⬚⬚ ⬚⬚⬚⬚ ⬚⬚⬚⬚ ⬚⬚⬚⬚

Expires End ⬚⬚ ⬚⬚   Security Code ⬚⬚⬚

Continued overleaf >>

| One off Special Gift to Waverley Abbey Trust | ☐ Please send me an acknowledgement of my gift | **B** | |

GRAND TOTAL (Total of A & B)

Gift Aid (your home address required, see overleaf)

giftaid it I am a UK taxpayer and want CWR to reclaim the tax on all my donations for the four years prior to this year **and on** all donations I make from the date of this Gift Aid declaration until further notice.*

Taxpayer's Full Name (in BLOCK CAPITALS) _____

Signature _____ **Date** _____

*I am a UK taxpayer and understand that if I pay less Income Tax and/or Capital Gains Tax than the amount of Gift Aid claimed on all my donations in that tax year it is my responsibility to pay any difference.

Your FREE Daily Bible Reading Notes Order

	Please Tick	FREE	£2 pcm	£5 pcm	£10 pcm	Other
Every Day with Jesus		☐	☐	☐	☐	☐ £ _____
Large Print *Every Day with Jesus*		☐	☐	☐	☐	☐ £ _____
Inspiring Women Every Day		☐	☐	☐	☐	☐ £ _____

All CWR Bible reading notes are also available in single issue **ebook** and **email subscription** format. Visit **waverleyabbeyresources.org** for further info.

CWR Instruction to your Bank or Building Society to pay by Direct Debit

DIRECT Debit

Please fill in the form and send to: CWR, Waverley Abbey House, Waverley Lane, Farnham, Surrey GU9 8EP

Name and full postal address of your Bank or Building Society

To: The Manager _____ Bank/Building Society

Address _____

_____

Postcode _____

Name(s) of Account Holder(s)

Branch Sort Code

Bank/Building Society Account Number

Originator's Identification Number

| 4 | 2 | 0 | 4 | 8 | 7 |

Reference

Instruction to your Bank or Building Society

Please pay CWR Direct Debits from the account detailed in this Instruction subject to the safeguards assured by the Direct Debit Guarantee. I understand that this Instruction may remain with CWR and, if so, details will be passed electronically to my Bank/Building Society.

Signature(s)

Date

Banks and Building Societies may not accept Direct Debit Instructions for some types of account

For a subscription outside of the UK please visit www.waverleyabbeyresources.org where you will find a list of our national distributors.

How would you like to hear from us? We would love to keep you up to date on all aspects of the CWR ministry, including; new publications, events & courses as well as how you can support us. .

If you **DO** want to hear from us on email, please tick here [ ] If you **DO NOT** want us to contact you by post, please tick here
You can update your preferences at any time by contacting our customer services team on 01252 784 700. You can view our privacy policy online at waverleyabbeyresources.org